Check Out Other Fun Books
by Jake Jokester!

For every occasion

Camping Edition

Winter &
Christmas Edition

Gamer's Edition

Travel Edition

How to Play
~The Rules~

- You need at least 2 players to play.

- Choose who will go first. The first player chooses a question for the next player (player 2) to answer.

- Player 2 chooses one answer out of the 2 options

> You cannot answer "both" or "neither".

Optional rule: the answering player has to explain why they made the choice that they made.

- The player who answered the last question becomes the next asker. If there are more than 2 players, you can either pick any person to answer the next question or you can just ask the person next to you, going around in a circle.

Most important rule: Laugh, smile and have lots of fun!

Warning

This book contains extra yucky, really gross, disgusting and very hilarious Would You Rather questions. Proceed with caution.

Recommended for ages 7+

Thanks for getting our book!

If you enjoy using it and it gives you lots of laughs and fun moments, we would appreciate your review on Amazon. Just head on over to this book's Amazon page and click "Write a customer review".

We read each and every one of them

Would You Rather...

babysit a cranky child for 3 hours

OR

listen to the cringey singing
of your aunt for 3 hours?

shave off your eyebrows and hair

OR

suck the blood and the
undigested food directly from the
stomach of a dead fish?

1

Would You Rather...

get thrown in front of
a lion in a cage

OR

challenge a raging bull in bull
fighting wearing red pants?

drink a glass of hot water with
20 teaspoons of pepper in it

OR

drink a glass of donkey milk?

2

Would You Rather...

present dog poo on a platter instead of a birthday cake to your friend on his/her birthday party

OR

gift her/him a ball of boogers that you've been collecting for 3 months?

drink a juice made from a rotting orange

OR

eat bread partially eaten up by rats?

drink a glass of someone's sweat

OR

eat a plate full of someone's hair?

eat someone else's ear wax

OR

use someone's saliva as
eye drops?

Would You Rather...

eat with your hands for a week
without being able to wash them

OR

not be able to wipe your butt
at all for a week?

have your breath smell like poop

OR

cry cat pee?

Would You Rather...

drink a glass of water
from a dirty fish tank

 OR

drink a cup of tea with a few
spider webs mixed into it?

poo in your bed everyday for a week
whilst lying in your bed by yourself

 OR

pee in your pants once
but in a public place?

Would You Rather...

never cut your hair

OR

never cut your nails?

bathe in elephant pee

OR

sleep on a pile of dog poo?

fart aloud in an elevator
full of people

OR

pee in the middle of
a bustling street?

eat someone else's booger

OR

lick an armpit?

Would You Rather...

eat a bowl of worms like spaghetti

OR

eat a bowl of cockroaches
with milk like cornfla es?

eat jam with pieces of
dead mice mixed in it

OR

drink coffee which has the blood
of a dead bat mixed in it?

Would You Rather...

eat only packaged food

OR

eat only raw food?

get caught by a tribe of
cannibals in the jungle

OR

get chased by a tiger?

Would You Rather...

smell someone's fart

OR

rub someone's mucus all over your palms to use it as moisturizer?

eat a burger from a trash can

OR

drink water from a glass used by a patient with a contagious disease?

Would You Rather...

have feathers all over

OR

have scaly skin like a crocodile?

lick dog saliva

OR

lick a live python?

Would You Rather...

drink a glass of drained water from a washing machine of a public laundry

OR

drink a glass of sink water left over from washing dishes in a restaurant?

drink a juice made from a rotting orange

OR

eat bread partially eaten up by rats?

Would You Rather...

eat french fries that were fried
in fish oil

OR

put a live small rat under your shirt?

have 300 cockroaches
under your bed sheets

OR

have 10 rats under
your bed sheets?

Would You Rather...

get stuck in a pool of thick coal tar

OR

run over a big sheet of glass
at a height of 15 feet which
might break any moment?

eat vanilla ice cream with
barbecue sauce

OR

eat a hamburger dipped
in sugar syrup?

Would You Rather...

after having a chewing gum, stick it in your girlfriend's/boyfriend's hair, laughing at her/him

OR

cut all the hair off your your girlfriend's/boyfriend's Pomeranian dog in front of her/him?

eat food that someone spat in

OR

drink water that someone spat in?

Would You Rather...

only drink

only eat?

eat a dead worm

OR

eat a dead fly?

eat the outer shell of a pineapple and throw away the pulp (the middle)

OR

eat the outer shell of a boiled egg and throw away the boiled egg?

chew and eat 5 teaspoons of pepper

OR

chew and eat 5 teaspoons of salt?

Would You Rather...

eat a pancake over which
a lizard just crawled over

OR

eat a bread over which a cockroach
has just been crawling on?

eat live earthworms

OR

eat live cockroaches?

Would You Rather...

always cut fruits and
vegetables using a sword

 OR

drink everything using a small spoon?

eat a rotten apple

 OR

eat a stale burger?

Would You Rather...

always cut fruits and
vegetables using a sword

OR

drink everything using a small spoon?

eat a rotten apple

OR

eat a stale burger?

eat a cake that's been sneezed on

OR

eat cake served by a hand which was not washed after cleaning the bathroom?

not eat for a month

OR

not poop for a month?

Would You Rather...

live with a troop of monkeys
in the jungle

 OR

in a skulk (group) of foxes?

kiss a poisonous snake

 OR

tickle a lion?

Would You Rather...

stick your hands in toilet water

OR

wash your face with a dirty
floor mop?

never brush your teeth

OR

never take baths or showers?

eat 3 tubes of toothpase

OR

drink a glass of chili water?

serve 20 years in prison for a crime committed by someone else

OR

be left alone without food and water in a jungle full of poisonous snakes, deadly mosquitoes and tigers?

Would You Rather...

dance barefoot on a floor
that has pieces of sharp
glass scattered all over

OR

sit on a chair made of hundreds
of pointy needles?

pee like a dog by lifting your
leg up at your neighbour's car
in front of him

OR

break into your neighbour's house
during the night whilst wearing
a mask and get caught?

eat a plate of uncooked rice

OR

eat a plate of rice cooked
in sewer water?

relieve yourself in an airport
toilet without no door

OR

have diarrhea in an 8 hour
long flight?

Would You Rather...

have an itchy armpit for
the next 3 months

OR

have a really smelly armpit
for the next 3 months?

lick your own spit

OR

ask a stranger to spit in your face?

Would You Rather...

break a raw egg gently on your girlfriend's/boyfriend's head unbenounced to him/her

OR

pour a glass of beer over her/his head head unbenounced to him/her?

never sleep

OR

never eat?

Would You Rather...

wash your face with toilet cleaner

OR

shampoo your hair with hen poo?

bite your fingernail

OR

bite your toenails?

run backwards on a busy street

OR

get pursued by a pack of dogs?

eat with your feet

OR

run a marathon on your hands?

eat a bread infested with worms

drink water full of leeches?

live in a cave next to the jungle

OR

live under a bridge in the city?

Would You Rather...

stay hungry for 5 days

OR

stay thirsty for 2 days?

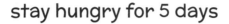

let your face get smeared with the
vomit of a baby sitting
next to you on a public bus

OR

get baby poo on your face whilst
its mom is change its diaper?

Would You Rather...

pee every time you stand up

OR

poop every time you sit down?

use a toothbrush which was just used few minutes ago for cleaning the teeth of a pig

OR

bathe using soap that was just used few minutes ago for bathing a dog with flees?

Would You Rather...

clean a public toilet
overflowing with poop

OR

clean a washbasin blocked
by lots of puke?

not drink a single drop
of water for 3 days

OR

not poo for 3 days?

roam the entire city without
pants but wearing underwear

 OR

go streaking in a football stadium
in the middle of a match?

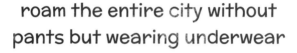

spend a night in a graveyard alone

OR

spend a night in a morgue alone?

Would You Rather...

poop mustard

OR

poop ketchup?

fall in a pit full of pus

OR

fall in a pit full of thorns?

Would You Rather...

put a hot iron on your cheek

hold a scorpion by
clasping your palms?

get married to a zombie

give birth and find out that your
child is a zombie?

Would You Rather...

drink milkshake with a heavy
dose of pepper in it

OR

drink coke with mentos in it?

spend a night in a dark
room with a snake

OR

with a tiger in a well-lit room?

Would You Rather...

eat pudding full of human nails

OR

drink coffee full of hair?

eat live butterflies

OR

eat dead grasshoppers?

Would You Rather...

wash your face with crow poo

OR

take a bath in cow dung?

never eat any fruits

OR

never eat any form of meat?

eat bread that has shoe polish on it

OR

drink coffee by mixing petrol in it?

eat a bowl of soup made
from used socks

OR

have a bowl of soup
made from sweat?

Would You Rather...

let a crow pick seeds off your head

OR

let a dog bite you?

drink snake blood

OR

chew and swallow a dead lizard?

wipe your food plate with
clean toilet paper but from
the toilet roll of a public toilet

OR

eat from the floor of a hospital?

eat 10 portions of food all at once

OR

stay hungry for 10 days?

Would You Rather...

kiss a bride at her marriage pushing her groom away

OR

slap the groom in the middle of the sermon?

eat toffee made of dog vomit

OR

eat a burger with a spread of saliva?

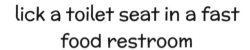

lick a toilet seat in a fast food restroom

OR

lick a toilet floor in a fast food restroom?

have an extra large belly

OR

have a 4 inch (10 cm) wide belly button?

Would You Rather...

eat a car tyre

OR

drink petrol?

---

eat raw food

OR

eat rotten food?

Would You Rather...

eat pure but raw food

OR

eat impure but cooked food?

eat a muffin that tastes like poop

OR

eat poop that tastes like a muffin?

Would You Rather...

snuff out 25 burning matchsticks
with your forefinge   and thumb

OR

drop melting wax from a burning
candle on your forehead?

eat an uncut, raw, smelly fish

OR

eat cooked rat meat?

Would You Rather...

vomit from your balcony while
waving 'bye' to your guests

OR

pee from the balcony
whilst waving 'bye'?

eat a broccoli infested
with caterpillars

OR

eat bread infested with worms?

Would You Rather...

put a live crab in your pants

OR

put a live snake around your neck?

eat live mosquitoes

OR

eat super moldy bread?

Would You Rather...

step on dog's poop with
your new sneakers

OR

step on human poop with
your new sneakers?

get bit by a
venomous king cobra

OR

get swallowed alive
by an anaconda?

Would You Rather...

get pecked on head by a woodpecker

OR

get bitten on the neck
by a vampire bat?

eat with the spoon used by
someone else in a restaurant

OR

eat a burger that has
sand mixed in it?

Would You Rather...

get bitten by a stray dog

OR

have three crows attack your head?

live in a zoo

OR

live in a railway station?

sniff a dog's butt

OR

sniff a cat's butt?

stay thirsty in the middle of a desert

OR

drink your own pee in the middle of
the dessert to quench your thirst?

Would You Rather...

gargle from the shaving bowl
that contains shaved hair,
shaving cream and water

OR

shampoo your hair with cat pee?

wear soiled and used
underpants as a bandana

OR

wear someone else's unwashed
soiled underwear?

Would You Rather...

have fur all over your body

OR

have two massive horns on your head?

ask your friend to smell your unwashed socks if he/she really is your friend

OR

ask her/him to brush his/her teeth with your saliva if she/he really is your friend?

Would You Rather...

sniff someone's underarm

OR

sniff someone's used socks?

eat raw chicken

OR

eat cooked python?

Would You Rather...

drink coffee that
has 25 dead flies in it

OR

eat spaghetti with a sauce that
has crushed cockroaches in it?

serve dog food at your birthday
party and declare aloud that all
who are present deserve this

OR

offer your teacher to buy
the test answers for the
price of 5 snickers bars?

59

Would You Rather...

use a broken toilet full of poo

OR

use a sink whish is full of someone else's vomit?

dive in a pool full of snakes

OR

dive in a pool full of cow poo?

Would You Rather...

eat a banana partially
eaten by a monkey

OR

eat a boiled egg partially
eaten by a dog?

eat live mosquitoes

OR

chew dung beetles?

Would You Rather...

drink the milk from the same bowl
from which a dog has drunk

eat food from the same bowl
from which a pig has eaten?

run in your school corridors
continuously flapping your hands
and yelling, "I am Batman/Batgirl"

OR

run in your school corridors
continuously jumping with a raised fist
yelling, "I am Superman/Supergirl"?

Would You Rather...

eat without washing your hands
after picking dog flees

OR

eat without washing your
hands after a cow licked your
hands whilst you fed it?

have a hippopotamus's
butt for a face

OR

have an elephant's butt
instead of your own?

Would You Rather...

sit in a plane next to a person
who is continuously farting

OR

sit on a bus next to a lady whose
dog has really bad diarrhea?

attend the Rouketopolemos rocket
apply dog's pee as perfume

OR

apply dog poo as a scrub
on your face?

lick a lollypop on which a bunch
of flies have just sat on

OR

lick a lollypop on which
someone has just sneezed?

drink a coffee with pigeon
poo as cream

OR

drink a coffee inside which was
made with water and cat pee?

Would You Rather...

eat your own poop
as rabbits do

OR

eat your own vomit
as dogs do?

unleash 20 snakes
in your classroom

OR

unleash 100 wasps
in your classroom?

Would You Rather...

let someone make noise
at your ear by continuously
biting a steel saucer

OR

let someone yell in your ear?

bathe with water
mixed with cat urine

OR

bathe with regular water but
using cat poo as soap?

Would You Rather...

ask someone to spit in your palms and rub it till it vanishes and then smell your palms

OR

ask a kid to spit out the chewing gum that he/she has been chewing and then you put it in your mouth and walk away?

play with dog vomit as slime

OR

play with human mucus as slime?

hold a baby that has
pooped its diaper

OR

hold a baby that has vomited
all over its clothes?

unclog a clogged toilet
with your bare hands

OR

unclog a sink full of vomit
with your bare hands?

Would You Rather...

eat on a plate which has not been cleaned and has food remains stuck on it

OR

drink a glass of water in which a waiter dipped each of his 10 fingers?

wear someone else's used underwear for a whole day

OR

squeeze a dog poo very hard for 10 seconds?

Would You Rather...

eat from unwashed dishes

OR

drink from a used glass?

let a monkey fart on your face

OR

stay in a room where 100 have farted in the last minute?

Would You Rather...

eat a cake at your best friend's birthday party and declare aloud that this is the most horrible cake you ever ate in your life

OR

steal birthday presents from your best friend's on his/ her birthday party?

clean hen droppings in a poultry farm

OR

clean cow poo in a cattle farm?

Would You Rather...

spend a day in a manure farm
where manure is prepared
by the animal excreta

OR

spend a day in a
slaughterhouse/abattoir?

lick the wet fur
of a newly born kitten

OR

lick a slimy fish?

Would You Rather...

pull ticks from a street/stray dog's fur with your teeth

OR

paint your room walls with dog poo and show it proudly to your parents?

be in a situation where you're caught mocking your teacher, not knowing that he/she is watching

OR

go to the principal's office and start dancing on his/her table while the principal is looking at you in a state of shock?

Would You Rather...

drink spilled coffee from
the restaurant floor

OR

eat noodles that fell on
someone's shoes?

brush your teeth using
someone else's toothbrush

OR

brush your teeth with your own
toothbrush but first brush it
across the inside of a toilet bowl?

eat stale fruits

OR

eat moldy bread?

change a baby's filthy
diaper with your hands

OR

hold a snot filled handkerchief
of a kid in your hands?

eat chocolate with dead
cockroaches in it

OR

eat marshmallows
dipped in goat poo?

clear & unclog the jammed
plumbing system in your home

OR

clean public toilets?

Would You Rather...

get wet in the rain of vomit

OR

get wet in the rain of pee?

brush your teeth using crow
poo as toothpaste

OR

shampoo your hair
with pig pee?

Would You Rather...

put your feet in a bathtub
full of leeches

OR

put a live non-poisonous snake
around your neck and keep it
there for a whole hour?

let a rat crawl
over your face

OR

let a spider crawl
inside your clothes?

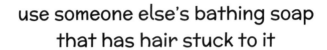
Would You Rather...

use someone else's bathing soap
that has hair stuck to it

OR

wear someone else's sweat-
soaked socks?

carry someone's feces in a
beaker for a lab test

OR

carry someone's urine in a
test tube for a lab test?

Would You Rather...

tell your principal that you have named your dog after him/her

OR

ask your teacher in front of the whole class whether he/she happy with his/her marriage?

eat candy made of dog saliva

OR

eat a jelly bean made of human mucus?

lie in an empty bathtub and let hundreds of spiders crawl all over your body

OR

lie in an empty bathtub and let hundreds of snakes crawl all over your body?

swallow live cockroaches

OR

swallow live flies?

Would You Rather...

smell a dead dog
who died a week ago

OR

smell Elephant's fart?

drink a glass of donkey milk

OR

drink a glass of pig milk?

Would You Rather...

clean the corners of your
eyes with your own saliva

OR

eat your dried boogers by
peeling them off your nose?

inspect and analyze someone's
vomit for scientific purposes

OR

inspect and analyze someone's
poop for scientific purposes?

Would You Rather...

use fish oil as perfume

OR

use a liquid that makes you smell like farts as perfume?

fart in the mic in your school assembly

OR

shut the classroom door in your principal's face while he/she is entering the classroom?

wipe your face with someone else's sweat-soaked handkerchief

OR

after a shower, wipe your body with someone else's wet, used towel?

deflate a police car tire and get caught while doing so

OR

get caught by your neighbor while making your dog pee on his/her newspaper?

Would You Rather...

swallow 4 teaspoons of baby saliva

OR

swallow 1 live non-poisonous spider?

smell someone's uncleaned
& smelly socks

OR

smell someone's sweaty &
smelly underarms?

Would You Rather...

eat from a pack of uneaten potato chips that you found in a trash can

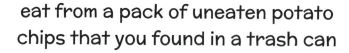

OR

eat a part of a worm-infested apple?

organize a competition in your class 'who can spit the farthest'

OR

organize an on-going competition in your class 'who can fart the loudest'?

Would You Rather...

run in your school corridors continuously shouting "I am crazzzy! woohoo!"

OR

run in your school corridors continuously declaring "I am too cool for school" to any person that passes by?

eat with a fork with which someone just scratched their butt

OR

eat cake from the hands of a child who just wiped the boogers off his nose?

Would You Rather...

decorate your room walls
with posters of vomit

OR

decorate your room walls
with posters of poop?

eat a pudding that has
human hair in it

OR

eat a burger that
has dead flies in it?

Would You Rather...

eat someone's nails

OR

eat dirt from sole
of someone's shoe?

walk barefoot on a floor
full of goat droppings

OR

walk barefoot on a floor
full of human vomit?

eat meatballs made from rat meat

OR

eat sausages made of earthworms?

eat dog meat stew in a
restaurant in China

OR

eat python meat stew in a
restaurant in Indonesia?

One last thing - we would love to hear
your feedback about this book!

If you found this activity book fun and useful, we
would be very grateful if you posted a short review on
Amazon! Your support does make a difference and we
read every review personally.

If you would like to leave a review, just head on
over to this book's Amazon page and click "Write a
customer review".

Thank you for your support!

Check Out Other Fun Books
by Jake Jokester!

For every occasion

Camping Edition

Winter &
Christmas Edition

Gamer's Edition

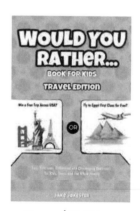

Travel Edition